Dominica

Everything You Need to Know

Copyright © 2024 by Noah Gil-Smith.

All rights reserved. No part of this book may be reproduced, distributed, or transmitted in any form or by any means, including photocopying, recording, or other electronic or mechanical methods, without the prior written permission of the publisher, except in the case of brief quotations embodied in critical reviews and certain other noncommercial uses permitted by copyright law. This book was created with the assistance of Artificial Intelligence. The content presented in this book is for entertainment purposes only. It should not be considered as a substitute for professional advice or comprehensive research. Readers are encouraged to independently verify any information and consult relevant experts for specific matters. The author and publisher disclaim any liability or responsibility for any loss, injury, or inconvenience caused or alleged to be caused directly or indirectly by the information presented in this book.

Introduction to Dominica 6

Geography and Climate of Dominica 8

A Brief History of Dominica: From Pre-Colonial Times to Independence 10

Indigenous Peoples of Dominica: Their Legacy and Influence 13

European Colonization of Dominica: A Story of Struggle and Resilience 15

Dominica's Role in the Caribbean Slave Trade: Impact and Legacy 18

The Fight for Freedom: Dominica's Journey to Independence 21

Modern-Day Dominica: Politics, Economy, and Society 23

Exploring Dominica's Breathtaking Landscapes: Mountains, Rivers, and Rainforests 25

Flora and Fauna of Dominica: Rich Biodiversity in a Small Island 27

Birdwatcher's Paradise: Avian Diversity in Dominica 29

Marine Life in Dominica: Diving into its Underwater Wonders 31

Creole Cuisine: A Culinary Journey Through Dominica's Flavors 33

From Sea to Plate: Fishing Traditions and Delicacies of Dominica 35

Exploring Dominica's Capital: Roseau, a Blend of History and Modernity 37

Portsmouth: A Coastal Gem with a Rich Maritime Heritage 40

Historic Forts of Dominica: Guardians of the Island's Past 43

Carib Territory: Preserving Indigenous Culture in Modern Times 46

Kalinago Heritage: Traditions, Arts, and Crafts 49

Music and Dance in Dominica: Soca, Calypso, and Bouyon Beats 52

Carnival in Dominica: A Colorful Celebration of Culture and Identity 55

Traditional Festivals and Celebrations in Dominica 58

Dominica's Literary Heritage: Writers and Poets from the Nature Isle 61

Visual Arts in Dominica: From Carib Petroglyphs to Contemporary Creations 64

The Language of Dominica: Creole, English, and Multilingualism 67

Education in Dominica: Nurturing Minds, Shaping Futures 69

Religion in Dominica: A Tapestry of Faiths and Beliefs 72

Healthcare System in Dominica: Providing Care in Paradise 74

Transportation in Dominica: Navigating the Island's Roads and Waters 77

Sustainable Tourism in Dominica: Balancing Preservation and Progress 80

Eco-Tourism Adventures: Hiking, Canyoning, and Nature Trails 83

Hot Springs and Wellness Tourism: Relaxation and Rejuvenation in Dominica 86

Dominica's Unique Accommodation: Eco-Lodges, Guesthouses, and Villas 89

Shopping and Souvenirs: Authentic Crafts and Local Products 91

Environmental Conservation in Dominica: Protecting the Nature Island 93

Community Development Initiatives in Dominica: Empowering Local Voices 96

Disaster Preparedness and Resilience in Dominica: Facing Nature's Fury 99

Future Prospects for Dominica: Challenges and Opportunities Ahead 102

Cultural Exchange and Volunteerism: Connecting with Dominica's Communities 105

Tips for Traveling to Dominica: Practical Advice for a Memorable Trip 108

Epilogue 112

Introduction to Dominica

In the heart of the Caribbean lies a hidden gem, the Nature Island of Dominica. Nestled between the French-speaking islands of Guadeloupe and Martinique, Dominica stands out for its unspoiled beauty, rugged landscapes, and vibrant culture. Known as the "Nature Island," Dominica boasts an abundance of natural wonders, from lush rainforests and cascading waterfalls to pristine beaches and volcanic peaks.

With a land area of just 290 square miles, Dominica may be small in size, but it packs a punch when it comes to biodiversity. Its rugged terrain, volcanic origin, and diverse microclimates have created a haven for rare and endemic species of flora and fauna. Dominica's rainforests are home to a myriad of plant and animal species, including the iconic Sisserou parrot, the national bird of Dominica, and the Jaco parrot.

The island's volcanic past is evident in its dramatic landscapes, with towering peaks like Morne Trois Pitons, a UNESCO World Heritage Site, dominating the skyline. Boiling Lake, one of the world's largest volcanic crater lakes, is a testament to Dominica's geothermal activity and draws adventurers from around the globe.

But Dominica's allure extends beyond its natural beauty. The island's rich history and vibrant culture add layers of complexity to its identity. Indigenous peoples inhabited Dominica long before European colonization, leaving behind traces of their heritage in the form of petroglyphs and archaeological sites.

European powers vied for control of Dominica during the colonial era, leading to periods of conflict and upheaval. The island passed between French and British hands multiple times before finally gaining independence in 1978. Today, remnants of colonial architecture and historic forts serve as reminders of Dominica's tumultuous past.

In addition to its natural and historical attractions, Dominica's cultural heritage is a source of pride for its people. The island's Afro-Caribbean and Kalinago (Carib) communities have preserved traditional customs, music, and cuisine, enriching Dominica's cultural tapestry. From vibrant Carnival celebrations to the rhythmic beats of traditional drumming, the spirit of Dominica is alive and thriving.

As we embark on a journey to discover all that Dominica has to offer, we'll delve deeper into its landscapes, history, culture, and people. From the heights of its volcanic peaks to the depths of its coral reefs, Dominica invites us to explore, learn, and connect with the essence of the Nature Island. So, join me as we uncover the wonders of Dominica, where nature reigns supreme and adventure awaits at every turn.

Geography and Climate of Dominica

Nestled in the Eastern Caribbean, Dominica is a captivating island nation renowned for its rugged landscapes and diverse ecosystems. Situated between Guadeloupe to the north and Martinique to the south, Dominica covers an area of approximately 290 square miles, making it one of the largest islands in the Lesser Antilles. Its geography is characterized by volcanic peaks, lush rainforests, and winding rivers, earning it the nickname "The Nature Island." The island's topography is dominated by a series of volcanic mountains, the most prominent being Morne Diablotins, which stands as the highest peak in Dominica at 4,747 feet (1,447 meters) above sea level. These volcanic formations have shaped the island's terrain, creating deep valleys, steep cliffs, and fertile slopes ideal for agriculture.

In addition to its mountainous interior, Dominica boasts a stunning coastline dotted with secluded coves, sandy beaches, and rugged cliffs. The island's shoreline stretches for approximately 148 miles (238 kilometers), offering ample opportunities for swimming, snorkeling, and exploring hidden bays. Dominica is renowned for its tropical climate, characterized by warm temperatures and high humidity throughout the year. The island experiences two distinct seasons: the dry season, which typically occurs from

December to May, and the rainy season, which lasts from June to November. During the rainy season, Dominica receives the bulk of its annual rainfall, with the mountainous interior receiving the highest precipitation levels. The island's climate is influenced by its location within the Caribbean hurricane belt, making it susceptible to tropical storms and hurricanes during the peak of the Atlantic hurricane season, which runs from June to November. While Dominica has experienced devastating storms in the past, including Hurricane Maria in 2017, the island's rugged terrain and proactive disaster preparedness measures have helped mitigate the impact of these natural disasters.

Despite its susceptibility to hurricanes, Dominica's lush vegetation thrives in its tropical climate, earning it a reputation as one of the most biodiverse islands in the Caribbean. The island is home to a wealth of flora and fauna, including rare and endemic species found nowhere else on Earth. Its rainforests teem with life, from colorful birds and butterflies to exotic plants and medicinal herbs.

In summary, Dominica's geography and climate play a defining role in shaping the island's natural beauty, biodiversity, and way of life. From its volcanic peaks to its pristine beaches, the Nature Island invites visitors to explore its diverse landscapes and experience the wonders of the Caribbean.

A Brief History of Dominica: From Pre-Colonial Times to Independence

The history of Dominica is a tapestry woven with threads of indigenous culture, European colonization, and struggles for independence. Long before the arrival of European explorers, the island was inhabited by indigenous peoples, including the Kalinago (Caribs) and the Taino. These Amerindian communities lived off the land, fishing, hunting, and cultivating crops like cassava and yams.

In 1493, Christopher Columbus made landfall on Dominica during his second voyage to the New World. He named the island "Dominica" after the Latin word for Sunday, the day of the week on which he sighted it. Despite Columbus' claim, European colonization did not begin in earnest until the 17th century when French and British settlers established rival colonies on the island.

Throughout the 17th and 18th centuries, Dominica became a battleground for European powers vying for control of the lucrative sugar trade. The island's rugged terrain and resistance from indigenous peoples made it difficult to conquer, leading to a series of conflicts between the French and British. Dominica changed hands multiple times during this period, with the Treaty of Paris in 1763 ultimately ceding the island to Great Britain.

Under British rule, Dominica experienced a boom in sugar production fueled by enslaved labor imported from Africa. The institution of slavery brought immense suffering to the island's African population, leading to slave rebellions and resistance movements. In 1834, slavery was officially abolished in the British Empire, but the legacy of slavery continued to shape Dominica's society and economy.

In the late 19th and early 20th centuries, Dominica underwent significant social and political changes. The island transitioned from a sugar-based economy to one focused on agriculture, with bananas emerging as the primary export crop. This shift brought increased prosperity to some, but the majority of Dominicans continued to live in poverty.

Calls for greater autonomy and self-governance grew louder in the early 20th century, culminating in the establishment of the West Indies Federation in 1958. Dominica became an associated state of the federation, gaining limited self-government. However, the federation was short-lived, and in 1967, Dominica withdrew and opted for full independence.

On November 3, 1978, Dominica achieved independence from Great Britain, becoming a sovereign nation within the Commonwealth. The island adopted a parliamentary democracy, with a president as head of state and a prime minister as head of government. Despite facing numerous challenges, including natural disasters and economic instability, Dominica has remained resilient, forging its path forward as a proud and independent nation in the Caribbean.

Indigenous Peoples of Dominica: Their Legacy and Influence

The indigenous peoples of Dominica, namely the Kalinago, also known as Caribs, and the Taino, have left an indelible mark on the island's history and culture. Long before European colonization, these Amerindian communities thrived on the lush landscapes of Dominica, living in harmony with nature and leaving behind a legacy that endures to this day.

The Kalinago were the dominant indigenous group on the island, known for their seafaring skills and warrior culture. They were skilled navigators and traders, traveling throughout the Caribbean and interacting with other indigenous peoples. The Kalinago lived in villages scattered across Dominica, building their homes from wood and palm leaves and cultivating crops like cassava, maize, and sweet potatoes.

The Taino, while less numerous than the Kalinago, also inhabited Dominica and contributed to the island's cultural tapestry. They were known for their pottery, agriculture, and spirituality, worshiping deities like Yucahu, the god of cassava, and Atabey, the mother goddess. Both the Kalinago and Taino practiced animistic religions, believing in the spiritual significance of natural phenomena like rivers, mountains, and animals. They conducted rituals and ceremonies to honor their gods and ancestors, often accompanied by music, dance, and storytelling. The arrival of European explorers, beginning with Christopher Columbus in 1493, marked a turning point for the indigenous peoples of Dominica. European colonization brought disease, warfare, and forced labor, decimating indigenous populations and disrupting their way of life. Many Kalinago and Taino were enslaved or killed, while others were forcibly removed from their ancestral lands.

Despite centuries of adversity, the Kalinago people have persevered and maintained a strong sense of cultural identity. Today, the Kalinago Territory in northeastern Dominica serves as a cultural and political center for the Kalinago people, preserving traditions, language, and customs passed down through generations. The legacy of the indigenous peoples of Dominica is evident in the island's place names, language, cuisine, and traditions. Words of Kalinago origin, such as "canoe" and "hammock," are still used in everyday language, while traditional foods like cassava bread and pepperpot stew remain staples of Dominican cuisine.

Efforts to preserve and celebrate indigenous culture are ongoing, with initiatives to revitalize traditional crafts, promote eco-tourism in the Kalinago Territory, and educate younger generations about their heritage. Through these efforts, the legacy and influence of the indigenous peoples of Dominica continue to shape the island's identity and enrich its cultural tapestry.

European Colonization of Dominica: A Story of Struggle and Resilience

The European colonization of Dominica is a tale of conquest, conflict, and cultural exchange that shaped the island's history for centuries. From the early encounters with Spanish explorers to the rivalry between French and British settlers, Dominica's colonial past is marked by struggle and resilience.

Spanish explorer Christopher Columbus was among the first Europeans to set foot on Dominica during his second voyage to the New World in 1493. He claimed the island for Spain, but it wasn't until the 17th century that European colonization efforts gained momentum. French and British settlers established rival colonies on the island, seeking to exploit its fertile land and strategic location in the Caribbean.

The French were the first to establish a permanent settlement on Dominica in the early 17th century, founding the town of Roseau and cultivating sugarcane plantations with enslaved African labor. However, their efforts were met with resistance from both indigenous peoples and rival European powers.

The British, eager to expand their colonial holdings in the Caribbean, seized control of Dominica multiple times during the 18th century, leading to a series of conflicts with the French. The island changed hands several times between the two colonial powers, with treaties like the Treaty of Paris in 1763 and the Treaty of Versailles in 1783 shaping its colonial borders.

Throughout this period, Dominica's indigenous population faced displacement, enslavement, and violence at the hands of European colonizers. The Kalinago people, in particular, fiercely resisted European encroachment, launching attacks on colonial settlements and retreating into the island's interior to preserve their way of life.

The abolition of slavery in the British Empire in 1834 brought significant changes to Dominica's colonial society, as former enslaved individuals gained freedom and rights. However, the legacy of slavery continued to shape the island's economy and social structure for generations to come.

In the late 19th and early 20th centuries, Dominica experienced a shift away from sugar production towards agriculture, with bananas emerging as the primary export crop. This transition brought economic prosperity to some, but inequalities persisted, with wealth concentrated in the hands of a few plantation owners and merchants.

Calls for greater autonomy and self-governance grew louder in the early 20th century, leading to the establishment of the West Indies Federation in 1958. Dominica became an associated state of the federation, gaining limited self-government before ultimately achieving independence from Great Britain on November 3, 1978.

Despite the challenges of colonization and exploitation, Dominica's people have shown remarkable resilience and determination to preserve their cultural heritage and forge their path forward as a sovereign nation in the Caribbean. Today, the island's diverse population and vibrant culture stand as a testament to its rich and complex history of struggle and resilience.

Dominica's Role in the Caribbean Slave Trade: Impact and Legacy

Dominica's role in the Caribbean slave trade is a sobering chapter in the island's history, one that leaves a lasting impact on its society and culture to this day. Like many other Caribbean islands, Dominica became a center for the transatlantic slave trade during the colonial era, as European powers sought to exploit the labor of enslaved Africans to cultivate lucrative crops like sugar, tobacco, and coffee.

The institution of slavery was deeply entrenched in Dominica's colonial economy, with enslaved Africans forced to work on plantations under brutal conditions. These enslaved individuals endured unimaginable hardships, including long hours of labor, harsh treatment, and separation from their families and communities.

The demand for enslaved labor in Dominica was fueled by the island's fertile land and favorable climate for agriculture. Sugar became the primary crop grown on the island's plantations, with profits from the sugar trade driving economic growth and prosperity for European colonizers.

The impact of the slave trade on Dominica's society was profound, shaping its demographics, culture, and social structure for centuries. Enslaved Africans brought with them diverse cultural traditions, languages, and religions, which influenced the development of creole languages, music, and religious practices on the island.

Resistance to slavery was widespread among enslaved Africans in Dominica, with numerous slave revolts and rebellions occurring throughout the colonial period. These acts of resistance ranged from individual acts of defiance to large-scale uprisings, challenging the authority of plantation owners and colonial authorities.

One of the most significant slave revolts in Dominica's history was the 1813 rebellion led by enslaved Africans on the Hampstead Estate. The rebellion, known as the "Hampstead Rebellion," was brutally suppressed by colonial forces, resulting in the execution of rebel leaders and the further entrenchment of slavery on the island.

The abolition of slavery in the British Empire in 1834 marked a turning point in Dominica's history, bringing an end to the institution of slavery and granting freedom to thousands of enslaved individuals. However, the legacy of slavery continued to shape the island's society and economy in the years that followed, as former enslaved individuals faced discrimination, poverty, and social exclusion.

Despite the abolition of slavery, the impact of the transatlantic slave trade on Dominica's society and culture cannot be understated. The legacy of slavery continues to be felt in issues of race, inequality, and social justice, highlighting the ongoing need for reconciliation, education, and awareness of this dark chapter in the island's history.

The Fight for Freedom: Dominica's Journey to Independence

The journey to independence for Dominica was marked by a combination of political activism, social movements, and international pressures. Following centuries of colonial rule under both French and British powers, the people of Dominica began to demand greater autonomy and self-governance in the mid-20th century.

Calls for independence gained momentum in the years following World War II, as colonial subjects across the Caribbean and Africa sought to assert their rights and aspirations for self-determination. In Dominica, political parties like the Dominica Labour Party (DLP) and the Dominica Freedom Party (DFP) emerged as advocates for independence, mobilizing support among the local population.

The West Indies Federation, established in 1958 as a precursor to Caribbean unity and self-government, provided an opportunity for Dominica to gain greater autonomy within a regional framework. However, the federation was short-lived, collapsing in 1962 due to internal tensions and disagreements among member states. In 1967, Dominica opted to become an associated state of the United Kingdom, gaining limited self-government while remaining part of the Commonwealth. This move towards greater autonomy marked a significant step towards eventual independence, as Dominicans began to assert their right to govern themselves free from external colonial control.

The road to independence was not without challenges, however. Internal divisions, political rivalries, and economic instability posed obstacles to the island's aspirations for self-rule. Additionally, external factors such as the Cold War and geopolitical tensions in the region influenced the trajectory of Dominica's independence movement.

On November 3, 1978, Dominica achieved full independence from Great Britain, becoming a sovereign nation within the Commonwealth. The island adopted a parliamentary democracy, with a president as head of state and a prime minister as head of government. Independence Day celebrations marked a historic moment of pride and celebration for the people of Dominica, as they embarked on a new chapter in their nation's history.

Since gaining independence, Dominica has faced numerous challenges, including natural disasters, economic instability, and social inequality. However, the spirit of resilience and determination that characterized the island's journey to independence continues to inspire its people as they work towards building a brighter future for generations to come.

Modern-Day Dominica: Politics, Economy, and Society

In modern-day Dominica, the dynamics of politics, economy, and society interplay to shape the island's identity and trajectory. Politically, Dominica operates under a parliamentary democracy, with a president as head of state and a prime minister as head of government. The political landscape is characterized by a multi-party system, with the Dominica Labour Party (DLP) and the United Workers Party (UWP) being the major political players.

Economically, Dominica's primary industries include agriculture, tourism, and services. Agriculture remains an important sector, with bananas, citrus fruits, and coconuts being the main export crops. Tourism has emerged as a significant contributor to the economy, driven by the island's natural beauty, eco-tourism attractions, and citizenship by investment program. Additionally, Dominica has made strides in developing its services sector, particularly in areas such as offshore banking and financial services.

Societally, Dominica is a melting pot of cultures, with influences from African, European, and indigenous traditions. The population is predominantly of African descent, with smaller percentages of European, indigenous, and mixed-race heritage. Religion plays a significant role in

Dominican society, with Christianity being the predominant faith, encompassing Catholicism, Protestantism, and other denominations. Traditional cultural practices, such as music, dance, and cuisine, are celebrated alongside modern influences, creating a vibrant and dynamic cultural landscape.

Challenges persist in modern-day Dominica, including issues such as unemployment, poverty, and environmental sustainability. The island's economy is susceptible to external shocks, including natural disasters and fluctuations in global markets. In recent years, Dominica has faced the devastating impact of hurricanes, such as Hurricane Maria in 2017, which highlighted the urgent need for disaster preparedness and resilience-building efforts.

Despite these challenges, Dominica remains resilient and resourceful, with a strong sense of community and national pride. Efforts to diversify the economy, promote sustainable development, and invest in education and infrastructure are underway, aimed at fostering long-term growth and prosperity for all Dominicans. As the island continues to navigate the complexities of the modern world, its rich history, diverse culture, and natural beauty serve as pillars of strength and resilience, guiding Dominica towards a brighter future.

Exploring Dominica's Breathtaking Landscapes: Mountains, Rivers, and Rainforests

Exploring Dominica's breathtaking landscapes is like stepping into a world of natural wonders that captivate the senses and leave an indelible mark on the soul. The island's rugged terrain, characterized by majestic mountains, winding rivers, and lush rainforests, offers an unparalleled opportunity for adventure and discovery.

Dominica's mountainous interior is dominated by a series of volcanic peaks, the most notable of which is Morne Diablotins, standing at 4,747 feet (1,447 meters) above sea level. These volcanic formations create a dramatic backdrop for the island's landscapes, providing sweeping vistas and challenging hiking trails for outdoor enthusiasts.

The rivers of Dominica are a lifeline for the island, nourishing its fertile valleys and sustaining a diverse array of plant and animal life. The island is home to numerous freshwater streams and waterfalls, including the iconic Trafalgar Falls and Emerald Pool, which draw visitors from around the world with their crystal-clear waters and serene beauty. The crown jewel of Dominica's natural heritage is its pristine rainforests, which cover over 60% of the island's land area and are among the most intact in the Caribbean. These lush forests are teeming with biodiversity, harboring rare and endemic species of flora and fauna found nowhere else on Earth. Visitors can explore winding hiking trails that lead through dense jungle vegetation, past cascading waterfalls, and to hidden natural treasures waiting to be discovered. One of the most famous attractions in Dominica's rainforests is the UNESCO World Heritage Site of Morne Trois Pitons National Park, home to iconic landmarks such as the Boiling Lake, the Valley of Desolation, and the Middleham Falls. This protected area showcases the island's geological and ecological diversity, offering a glimpse into the raw power and beauty of nature.

In addition to its mountains, rivers, and rainforests, Dominica boasts a diverse array of ecosystems, including coastal mangroves, coral reefs, and volcanic hot springs. These natural features provide habitat for a wide variety of marine life, making Dominica a popular destination for snorkeling, diving, and eco-tourism activities.

Exploring Dominica's breathtaking landscapes is not just about admiring the beauty of nature; it's about immersing oneself in an environment that inspires awe, wonder, and reverence for the natural world. Whether trekking through dense jungle, bathing in crystal-clear rivers, or marveling at volcanic peaks, the experience of exploring Dominica's landscapes is nothing short of transformative, leaving visitors with memories that will last a lifetime.

Flora and Fauna of Dominica: Rich Biodiversity in a Small Island

In the small island of Dominica lies an astonishing richness of flora and fauna, making it a biodiversity hotspot in the Caribbean. Despite its modest size, Dominica boasts an impressive array of ecosystems, ranging from lush rainforests and coastal mangroves to volcanic peaks and coral reefs. This diverse landscape provides habitat for a staggering variety of plant and animal species, many of which are endemic to the island.

Dominica's rainforests are among the most intact in the Caribbean, harboring an abundance of flora, including towering hardwood trees, ferns, orchids, and bromeliads. The dense canopy of these forests creates a haven for wildlife, with numerous species of birds, mammals, reptiles, and amphibians thriving in the understory. Among the most iconic inhabitants of Dominica's rainforests are its parrots, including the rare and endangered Sisserou parrot, which is the national bird of Dominica. In addition to its rainforests, Dominica is home to a wealth of freshwater ecosystems, including rivers, streams, and waterfalls. These waterways provide habitat for numerous species of fish, crustaceans, and aquatic plants, as well as serving as important breeding grounds for migratory birds. Dominica's rivers are also known for their unique geological features, such as natural hot springs, sulfur vents, and underwater caves.

Along its coastline, Dominica's marine environments are equally diverse, with coral reefs, seagrass beds, and mangrove forests supporting a rich array of marine life. The island's coral reefs are teeming with colorful fish, sea turtles, and invertebrates, while its mangrove forests provide essential nursery habitat for juvenile fish and crustaceans. Dominica's coastal waters are also frequented by whales, dolphins, and other marine mammals, making it a popular destination for eco-tourism and whale watching.

Despite its relatively small land area, Dominica boasts an impressive number of endemic species, many of which are found nowhere else on Earth. These include plants like the Bois Cotlette tree and the Dominican flag flower, as well as animals like the Dominican green anole and the Dominican ground lizard. The island's isolation, rugged terrain, and diverse microclimates have contributed to the evolution of these unique species over millions of years.

Efforts to conserve Dominica's rich biodiversity are ongoing, with initiatives aimed at protecting critical habitats, preserving endangered species, and promoting sustainable land use practices. By safeguarding its natural heritage, Dominica seeks to ensure that future generations can continue to marvel at the astonishing richness of flora and fauna that call this small island home.

Birdwatcher's Paradise: Avian Diversity in Dominica

For bird enthusiasts, Dominica is nothing short of a paradise. Nestled in the heart of the Caribbean, this lush island boasts an astonishing diversity of avian species, making it a haven for birdwatchers from around the world. With its varied ecosystems, ranging from dense rainforests and coastal mangroves to rugged mountains and freshwater rivers, Dominica provides habitat for an impressive array of birds, both resident and migratory.

One of the most iconic birds of Dominica is the Sisserou parrot, also known as the Imperial parrot, which is the national bird of the island. Endemic to Dominica, this majestic bird is recognized by its vibrant green plumage, bold red breast, and distinctive curved beak. The Sisserou parrot is highly prized by birdwatchers for its rarity and beauty, and sightings of this elusive species are considered a highlight of any birdwatching excursion on the island.

In addition to the Sisserou parrot, Dominica is home to a diverse range of other bird species, including numerous endemic and migratory birds. Among the most notable residents are the Jaco parrot, the red-necked pigeon, and the purple-throated carib, each of which adds to the rich tapestry of avian life on the island.

Dominica's rainforests are particularly rich in birdlife, with countless species of songbirds, hummingbirds, and raptors flitting among the dense foliage. Visitors to the island's interior can expect to encounter a symphony of bird calls, from the melodious songs of thrushes and warblers to the haunting cries of hawks and owls.

Along the coast, mangrove forests provide habitat for waterbirds such as herons, egrets, and kingfishers, while coral reefs attract seabirds like pelicans, terns, and frigatebirds. Inland waterways, including rivers, streams, and waterfalls, are frequented by waterfowl such as ducks, herons, and gallinules, adding to the diversity of birdlife in Dominica.

Birdwatching in Dominica is not just about ticking off species from a list; it's about immersing oneself in the sights and sounds of nature, connecting with the environment, and experiencing the thrill of discovery. Whether exploring the rainforests of Morne Trois Pitons National Park, birding along the shores of Cabrits National Park, or simply enjoying the birdlife in the gardens and forests of Dominica's towns and villages, birdwatchers are sure to be captivated by the avian wonders of this Caribbean paradise.

Marine Life in Dominica: Diving into its Underwater Wonders

Diving into the waters surrounding Dominica is like entering a vibrant underwater world teeming with life and color. Situated in the Eastern Caribbean, this small island boasts an incredible diversity of marine life, making it a paradise for snorkelers and scuba divers alike. Dominica's marine ecosystems, ranging from coral reefs and seagrass beds to volcanic vents and underwater caves, provide habitat for a staggering array of species, both large and small.

One of the highlights of diving in Dominica is exploring its coral reefs, which are home to an abundance of marine organisms, including colorful fish, crustaceans, and invertebrates. The reefs are composed of hard and soft corals, forming intricate structures that provide shelter and food for a variety of reef-dwelling creatures. Divers can expect to encounter species such as parrotfish, angelfish, butterflyfish, and moray eels, as well as larger predators like barracudas and reef sharks. In addition to its coral reefs, Dominica's underwater landscape features an array of other habitats, including seagrass beds, mangrove forests, and rocky outcrops. These habitats support a diverse range of marine life, including sea turtles, rays, octopuses, and lobsters. Seagrass beds are particularly important as nursery areas for juvenile fish and other marine organisms, providing shelter and food for young animals as they grow and mature.

One of the most unique aspects of diving in Dominica is the opportunity to explore its volcanic vents and underwater geothermal features. The island's volcanic origins have created a network of hot springs, sulfur vents, and underwater caves that are home to specialized organisms adapted to extreme environments. Divers can witness the bizarre and otherworldly landscapes of places like Champagne Reef, where geothermal activity releases streams of warm bubbles from the ocean floor, creating a surreal underwater experience.

Dominica's waters are also frequented by migratory species, including whales, dolphins, and sea birds. The island's strategic location in the Caribbean makes it an important stopover point for these animals as they travel between breeding and feeding grounds. Whale watching tours are a popular activity in Dominica, offering visitors the chance to observe humpback whales, sperm whales, and other cetaceans in their natural habitat.

Efforts to protect Dominica's marine ecosystems are ongoing, with initiatives aimed at conserving coral reefs, promoting sustainable fishing practices, and reducing pollution. By preserving its underwater wonders, Dominica seeks to ensure that future generations can continue to enjoy the beauty and biodiversity of its marine environment for years to come.

Creole Cuisine: A Culinary Journey Through Dominica's Flavors

Embarking on a culinary journey through Dominica means immersing oneself in the rich and flavorful world of Creole cuisine. Influenced by African, European, and indigenous traditions, Dominica's culinary heritage reflects the island's diverse cultural tapestry and natural abundance of fresh ingredients. From hearty stews and spicy seafood dishes to tropical fruits and aromatic spices, every meal in Dominica is a celebration of flavor and tradition.

One of the cornerstones of Creole cuisine in Dominica is the use of locally sourced ingredients, including fresh fruits, vegetables, herbs, and seafood. Staples such as plantains, yams, cassava, and breadfruit are commonly used in dishes like callaloo, a hearty soup made with leafy greens and coconut milk, and provisions, a dish featuring boiled root vegetables served with saltfish or meat.

Seafood plays a prominent role in Dominica's culinary repertoire, with the island's coastal waters teeming with a variety of fish, shellfish, and crustaceans. Lobster, crab, shrimp, and conch are popular ingredients in dishes like crab backs, a savory crabmeat stuffing served in crab shells, and seafood bouillon, a rich and flavorful stew made with a medley of fish and shellfish.

Spices and seasonings are essential to Creole cooking, adding depth and complexity to dishes with their bold flavors and aromas. Common spices used in Dominica include garlic, ginger, thyme, bay leaves, and Scotch bonnet peppers, which impart a fiery kick to many dishes. Other seasonings such as curry powder, allspice, and nutmeg are also used to enhance the taste of meats, stews, and marinades.

No culinary journey through Dominica would be complete without sampling the island's wide variety of tropical fruits and beverages. Mangoes, papayas, guavas, and passion fruit are just a few of the fruits that thrive in Dominica's fertile soil, providing a refreshing and nutritious addition to meals or snacks. Coconut water, rum punch, and sorrel are popular beverages enjoyed by locals and visitors alike, offering a taste of the island's vibrant and diverse culinary culture.

Throughout Dominica, traditional cooking methods such as stewing, grilling, and steaming are employed to create dishes that are both flavorful and nourishing. Meals are often prepared communally, with family and friends coming together to share food, stories, and laughter. This sense of community and hospitality is an integral part of Creole cuisine in Dominica, reflecting the warmth and generosity of the island's people.

From Sea to Plate: Fishing Traditions and Delicacies of Dominica

In Dominica, the connection between sea and plate is deeply ingrained in the island's culture and culinary traditions. Fishing has long been a vital part of life for coastal communities, providing sustenance, livelihoods, and a source of cultural identity. From the bountiful waters of the Caribbean Sea, fishermen haul in a rich bounty of fish, shellfish, and crustaceans, which find their way onto the tables of homes, restaurants, and markets across the island.

The fishing traditions of Dominica are as diverse as the marine ecosystems that surround the island. Traditional fishing methods such as handline fishing, net casting, and lobster trapping are still practiced by many fishermen, particularly in rural coastal villages. These methods, passed down through generations, rely on skill, knowledge of the tides, and a deep understanding of the sea to yield a successful catch. In addition to traditional fishing, Dominica is also home to a thriving commercial fishing industry, with modern fishing vessels equipped with advanced technology and equipment. Commercial fishermen target a variety of species, including tuna, mahi-mahi, snapper, and grouper, which are exported to markets both locally and internationally. The fishing industry plays a significant role in Dominica's economy, providing employment opportunities and contributing to the island's food security.

One of the most iconic delicacies of Dominica's fishing culture is the island's famed seafood bouillon, a hearty stew made with a medley of fish, shellfish, and vegetables. This dish, simmered slowly over an open fire or stove, is a favorite among locals and visitors alike, offering a taste of the sea's bounty in every spoonful. Other popular seafood dishes in Dominica include grilled lobster, fish cakes, crab backs, and shrimp creole, each showcasing the island's diverse culinary heritage.

In addition to fresh seafood, Dominica is also known for its preserved fish products, such as saltfish and smoked fish. Saltfish, also known as bacalao, is a staple ingredient in many Dominican dishes, including the traditional breakfast dish of saltfish and bakes. Smoked fish, often prepared using traditional smoking methods, adds a distinctive flavor to soups, stews, and salads, lending a taste of the sea to any dish.

Beyond its culinary significance, fishing holds a special place in the hearts of Dominicans, serving as a source of pride, tradition, and cultural heritage. Whether casting a line from the shore, hauling in a net from a fishing boat, or enjoying a seafood feast with friends and family, the sea continues to play a central role in the life and identity of the people of Dominica.

Exploring Dominica's Capital: Roseau, a Blend of History and Modernity

Nestled on the western coast of Dominica lies the vibrant capital city of Roseau, a charming blend of history and modernity that serves as the cultural and commercial hub of the island. With its colorful colonial architecture, bustling markets, and lively waterfront, Roseau offers visitors a glimpse into the rich tapestry of Dominican life and heritage.

The history of Roseau dates back to the 18th century when French settlers established the town as a trading post and administrative center. Over the years, Roseau grew into a thriving port city, serving as a hub for trade and commerce in the Caribbean. Today, remnants of its colonial past can be seen in the historic buildings and landmarks that dot the cityscape, including the Old Market Square, the Dominica Museum, and the Roseau Cathedral.

Despite its historical roots, Roseau is a city that embraces modernity, with bustling streets lined with shops, restaurants, and businesses. The city's vibrant atmosphere is fueled by its diverse population, which includes people of African, European, and indigenous descent, as well as immigrants from other Caribbean islands and beyond.

One of the highlights of exploring Roseau is strolling along its picturesque waterfront, where visitors can take in panoramic views of the Caribbean Sea and watch as fishing boats come and go from the harbor. The waterfront is also home to the bustling Roseau Market, where vendors sell fresh produce, spices, crafts, and other goods in a lively and colorful atmosphere.

In addition to its markets and waterfront, Roseau boasts a variety of cultural attractions and landmarks that showcase the city's unique heritage. The Dominica Botanic Gardens, established in the 18th century, are a peaceful oasis in the heart of the city, featuring lush tropical vegetation, towering trees, and colorful flower beds. The gardens are also home to the famous Sisserou parrot, the national bird of Dominica.

Another must-visit destination in Roseau is the Morne Bruce viewpoint, which offers stunning panoramic views of the city and surrounding landscape. From this vantage point, visitors can admire the rugged coastline, lush green hills, and historic landmarks that make Roseau such a special place.

Throughout Roseau, visitors will find a variety of restaurants, cafes, and eateries serving up a diverse array of culinary delights, from traditional Creole dishes to international cuisine. Whether dining on fresh seafood at a waterfront restaurant or sampling local street food at the market, visitors to Roseau are sure to find something to tantalize their taste buds.

With its blend of history, culture, and modern amenities, Roseau is a city that invites exploration and discovery, offering visitors a taste of Dominican life and hospitality at its finest. Whether wandering its historic streets, exploring its cultural landmarks, or simply soaking in the vibrant atmosphere, a visit to Roseau is an experience that will leave a lasting impression.

Portsmouth: A Coastal Gem with a Rich Maritime Heritage

Nestled on the northern coast of Dominica lies the picturesque town of Portsmouth, a coastal gem with a rich maritime heritage that dates back centuries. As the second-largest town on the island, Portsmouth has long been a hub of activity, serving as a center for trade, fishing, and boat building.

The history of Portsmouth is closely intertwined with its maritime roots, with the town originally founded by the British in the 18th century as a garrison town and naval base. Its strategic location along the coast made it an ideal port for ships traveling between Europe, the Caribbean, and the Americas, and it quickly became a bustling center of commerce and industry.

One of the most prominent landmarks in Portsmouth is Fort Shirley, a historic military fortification built by the British in the late 18th century to protect the island from potential invasion. Today, the fort is a UNESCO World Heritage Site and serves as a reminder of Portsmouth's colonial past, offering visitors a glimpse into the island's history and heritage.

In addition to its military history, Portsmouth is also known for its vibrant fishing industry, with the town's fishermen hauling in a bounty of fish, lobster, and other seafood from the waters of the Caribbean Sea. The Portsmouth Fisheries Complex, located along the waterfront, is a bustling hub where fishermen bring their catches to be sold at the local market or exported to markets abroad.

Portsmouth's maritime heritage is also reflected in its boat building tradition, with skilled craftsmen using traditional techniques to construct wooden boats and fishing vessels by hand. The town's shipyards are a hive of activity, with boats of all shapes and sizes taking shape under the skilled hands of local artisans.

Despite its historical roots, Portsmouth is a town that embraces modernity, with a variety of amenities and attractions catering to residents and visitors alike. The town's waterfront promenade is lined with shops, restaurants, and cafes, offering stunning views of the Caribbean Sea and nearby islands.

One of the highlights of visiting Portsmouth is exploring its surrounding natural beauty, with lush rainforests, pristine beaches, and scenic hiking trails all within easy reach. Nearby attractions such as the Indian River, Cabrits National Park, and the Syndicate Nature Trail provide opportunities for outdoor adventure and exploration, making Portsmouth an ideal destination for nature lovers and outdoor enthusiasts.

With its rich maritime heritage, stunning natural beauty, and warm hospitality, Portsmouth is a coastal gem that invites visitors to explore its history, culture, and natural wonders. Whether strolling along its historic streets, sailing the waters of the Caribbean Sea, or simply soaking in the laid-back island vibe, a visit to Portsmouth is sure to leave a lasting impression.

Historic Forts of Dominica: Guardians of the Island's Past

The historic forts of Dominica stand as silent sentinels, guardians of the island's past and reminders of its tumultuous history. From rugged coastal cliffs to lush mountaintops, these fortifications bear witness to centuries of conflict, colonization, and conquest, reflecting the strategic importance of Dominica in the Caribbean.

One of the most iconic forts in Dominica is Fort Shirley, located within Cabrits National Park on the northern tip of the island. Built by the British in the late 18th century, Fort Shirley was intended to defend Dominica from potential invasion by rival European powers. Today, the fort is a UNESCO World Heritage Site and offers visitors a glimpse into the island's colonial past, with well-preserved barracks, cannons, and defensive structures.

Another notable fortification in Dominica is Fort Young, located in the capital city of Roseau. Originally constructed by the British in the 18th century, Fort Young served as a key military outpost and played a significant role in defending Roseau from attacks by French and indigenous forces. Over the years, the fort has been renovated and repurposed, and today it serves as a luxury hotel and conference center, offering stunning views of the Caribbean Sea and Roseau's waterfront.

In addition to Fort Shirley and Fort Young, Dominica is home to a number of other historic forts and military installations, each with its own unique story to tell. Fort George, Fort Saint James, and Fort Rupert are just a few examples of the island's fortified landmarks, many of which have been preserved as heritage sites or tourist attractions.

The construction of these forts required significant labor and resources, with skilled craftsmen and enslaved laborers working together to build sturdy walls, bastions, and gun emplacements. The forts were strategically positioned to command key vantage points, such as harbor entrances, mountain passes, and coastal cliffs, allowing their defenders to repel enemy attacks and control access to the island.

Despite their military significance, many of Dominica's historic forts were eventually abandoned or fell into disrepair as the need for coastal defense waned in the 19th and 20th centuries. Today, efforts are underway to preserve and protect these valuable cultural heritage sites, with restoration projects, interpretive signage, and guided tours helping to educate visitors about their historical significance.

Visiting the historic forts of Dominica is not just about exploring ancient ruins; it's about connecting with the island's past, learning about its rich cultural heritage, and appreciating the ingenuity and resilience of those who built and defended these mighty fortifications. Whether standing atop a rampart, gazing out at the sea, or tracing the footsteps of soldiers who once marched within their walls, the forts of Dominica offer a window into the island's storied past and a testament to its enduring legacy.

Carib Territory: Preserving Indigenous Culture in Modern Times

Nestled in the lush hills of northeastern Dominica lies the Carib Territory, a vibrant community that serves as a living testament to the island's indigenous heritage. Home to the Kalinago people, who are descendants of the island's original Carib inhabitants, the Carib Territory is a place where traditional culture and modern life coexist in harmony.

The Carib Territory was established in 1903 by the British colonial authorities, who set aside land for the Kalinago people to preserve their way of life and cultural traditions. Today, the territory spans over 3,700 acres and is home to approximately 3,000 residents, making it one of the largest indigenous reserves in the Caribbean.

One of the most distinctive features of the Carib Territory is its traditional architecture, with many homes and buildings constructed using traditional materials and techniques. Thatched roofs, wooden walls, and earthen floors are common features of Kalinago homes, which are designed to blend seamlessly with the natural environment and withstand the tropical climate.

In addition to its traditional architecture, the Carib Territory is known for its vibrant cultural heritage, which is celebrated through music, dance, storytelling, and art. The Kalinago people have a rich oral tradition, with stories and legends passed down from generation to generation, preserving the history and wisdom of their ancestors.

One of the most iconic cultural events in the Carib Territory is the Kalinago Barana Aute, a cultural village and heritage site that showcases traditional Kalinago culture and craftsmanship. Visitors to the village can learn about traditional crafts such as basket weaving, pottery making, and cassava processing, as well as participate in cultural demonstrations and performances.

Despite its traditional roots, the Carib Territory is also a place of innovation and adaptation, with residents embracing modern amenities and technologies while still preserving their cultural identity. Many Kalinago people are involved in agriculture, fishing, and eco-tourism, using sustainable practices to maintain a connection with the land and sea that has sustained their community for generations.

One of the challenges facing the Carib Territory is the preservation of its cultural heritage in the face of modernization and globalization. Efforts are underway to document and safeguard traditional knowledge, language, and customs, as well as promote cultural exchange and education within the community and beyond.

Visiting the Carib Territory is not just about experiencing traditional culture; it's about connecting with a living, breathing community that is proud of its heritage and committed to preserving it for future generations. Whether exploring the lush rainforests, attending a cultural event, or simply engaging with residents and learning their stories, a visit to the Carib Territory offers a unique and enriching glimpse into the heart and soul of Dominica's indigenous culture.

Kalinago Heritage: Traditions, Arts, and Crafts

The Kalinago people, indigenous to Dominica, have a rich and vibrant cultural heritage that is celebrated through their traditions, arts, and crafts. Rooted in centuries of history and passed down through generations, Kalinago culture reflects a deep connection to the land, sea, and natural world.

One of the most prominent aspects of Kalinago heritage is their traditional crafts, which are crafted using age-old techniques and materials sourced from the surrounding environment. Basket weaving, in particular, is a skill that has been practiced by Kalinago women for centuries, with intricately woven baskets and trays crafted from locally sourced materials such as bamboo, palm leaves, and vines. These baskets are not only practical for carrying and storing goods but also serve as works of art, with each design and pattern holding symbolic meaning.

In addition to basket weaving, the Kalinago are also known for their pottery making, using clay dug from the riverbanks and fired using traditional methods. Kalinago pottery is characterized by its distinctive designs and motifs, which often incorporate geometric patterns, animal imagery, and symbols inspired by nature. These pottery pieces are not only functional but also serve as cultural artifacts, preserving the artistic traditions of the Kalinago people for future generations.

Another important aspect of Kalinago heritage is their music and dance, which are integral parts of their cultural identity and social gatherings. Traditional Kalinago music is characterized by rhythmic drumming, chanting, and singing, with songs often accompanied by traditional instruments such as the gomier drum, tambou, and shak-shak. Dance plays a central role in Kalinago ceremonies and celebrations, with dances such as the Bele and Jing Ping performed to commemorate important events and milestones in the community.

In addition to their traditional arts and crafts, the Kalinago people also have a rich oral tradition, with stories, legends, and myths passed down through generations. These stories often feature themes of nature, spirituality, and the ancestral past, providing insight into the beliefs, values, and worldview of the Kalinago people.

Despite the challenges of modernization and globalization, the Kalinago people remain committed to preserving their cultural heritage and passing it on to future generations. Efforts are underway to revitalize traditional crafts, promote cultural education and exchange, and empower Kalinago artisans and craftsmen to showcase their skills and talents on a wider stage.

Visitors to Dominica have the opportunity to experience Kalinago culture firsthand through cultural tours, workshops, and visits to the Kalinago Territory. By engaging with Kalinago artisans, learning about their traditions, and supporting their crafts, visitors can help to ensure the preservation and continuation of Kalinago heritage for years to come.

Music and Dance in Dominica: Soca, Calypso, and Bouyon Beats

Music and dance are deeply ingrained in the cultural fabric of Dominica, with a rich tapestry of rhythms, melodies, and movements that reflect the island's diverse heritage and vibrant spirit. From the pulsating beats of soca and calypso to the infectious energy of bouyon, Dominica's musical landscape is as diverse as its people, encompassing a wide range of genres and styles that celebrate life, love, and the rhythms of the Caribbean.

Soca music, with its infectious rhythms and catchy melodies, is a cornerstone of Dominica's musical identity. Originating in Trinidad and Tobago, soca has become immensely popular throughout the Caribbean, including Dominica, where it serves as the soundtrack to Carnival celebrations and other festive occasions. Characterized by its upbeat tempo, lively instrumentation, and infectious energy, soca music is all about getting people on their feet and moving to the beat.

Calypso music also holds a special place in Dominica's musical heritage, with its roots tracing back to the African and European influences that shaped the island's culture. Calypso songs are known for their witty lyrics, social commentary, and infectious rhythms, with themes ranging from politics and current events to love and romance. Calypso competitions, known as calypso tents, are a popular fixture during Carnival season, where local singers and performers showcase their talent and creativity on stage.

Bouyon music is another genre that has emerged from Dominica's musical melting pot, blending elements of soca, dancehall, reggae, and traditional Dominican rhythms to create a sound that is uniquely its own. Bouyon is characterized by its heavy basslines, pulsating rhythms, and energetic lyrics, with songs often celebrating the spirit of the Caribbean and the joys of life on the island. Bouyon has gained popularity not only in Dominica but also in other Caribbean countries and beyond, with artists such as Triple Kay International and WCK (Windward Caribbean Kulture) leading the way.

In addition to soca, calypso, and bouyon, Dominica is also home to a variety of other musical genres and styles, including reggae, dancehall, zouk, and traditional Dominican music such as jing ping and lapo kabwit. Music and dance are integral parts of daily life in Dominica, with festivals, concerts, and dance parties providing opportunities for people to come together, celebrate, and express themselves through music and movement.

Whether dancing to the infectious rhythms of soca, singing along to the witty lyrics of calypso, or grooving to the pulsating beats of bouyon, music and dance are essential elements of the Dominican experience, uniting people of all ages, backgrounds, and walks of life in a celebration of culture, community, and Caribbean pride.

Carnival in Dominica: A Colorful Celebration of Culture and Identity

Carnival in Dominica is not just a festival; it's a cultural extravaganza that brings the entire island to life with music, dance, and revelry. Held annually in the weeks leading up to Lent, Carnival is a vibrant celebration of Dominican culture, identity, and heritage, attracting locals and visitors alike from near and far to partake in the festivities.

The origins of Carnival in Dominica can be traced back to the island's colonial past, with the festival evolving over time to incorporate elements of African, European, and indigenous traditions. Today, Carnival is a colorful and dynamic expression of Dominican culture, featuring a mix of music, dance, costume, and pageantry that reflects the island's rich cultural tapestry.

One of the highlights of Carnival in Dominica is the music, with soca, calypso, and bouyon providing the soundtrack to the festivities. Throughout Carnival season, the streets of Dominica come alive with the sounds of steel drums, brass bands, and live performances, as musicians and singers entertain crowds with infectious rhythms and catchy melodies.

Dance is another integral part of Carnival in Dominica, with vibrant parades, street parties, and dance competitions taking place throughout the island. From traditional dances such as the Bele and Jing Ping to modern choreography inspired by hip-hop and dancehall, Carnival is a time for people of all ages to let loose, express themselves, and revel in the joy of movement.

Costume design is a major aspect of Carnival in Dominica, with elaborate masquerade costumes and headdresses adorned with feathers, sequins, and beads. Each costume tells a story, with themes ranging from historical events and cultural icons to fantasy and mythology. Participants spend months designing and creating their costumes, often working in teams or groups to bring their vision to life.

The crowning jewel of Carnival in Dominica is the Grand Parade, a dazzling spectacle of color, music, and creativity that winds its way through the streets of Roseau. Floats adorned with intricate designs and motifs glide alongside masqueraders in elaborate costumes, while spectators line the streets to cheer, dance, and soak in the atmosphere.

In addition to the Grand Parade, Carnival in Dominica also features a variety of other events and activities, including calypso competitions, steel pan concerts, and beauty pageants. Each event adds its own unique flavor to the Carnival experience, showcasing the talent, creativity, and diversity of the Dominican people.

But Carnival in Dominica is more than just a celebration; it's a time for reflection, renewal, and unity. As the island comes together to celebrate its culture and heritage, Carnival serves as a reminder of the resilience and spirit of the Dominican people, who have overcome adversity and hardship to create a vibrant and inclusive festival that welcomes all to join in the fun and festivities.

Traditional Festivals and Celebrations in Dominica

In addition to Carnival, Dominica is home to a variety of traditional festivals and celebrations that showcase the island's rich cultural heritage and vibrant community spirit. From religious observances to harvest festivals, these events offer a unique glimpse into Dominican life and traditions.

One of the most important traditional festivals in Dominica is the Feast of La Marguerite, also known as La Marguerite Festival. Held annually on the first Sunday in May, this religious celebration honors Saint Margaret Mary Alacoque, the patron saint of Dominica. The festival features a colorful procession, Mass at the Catholic Church, and cultural performances, drawing locals and visitors alike to participate in the festivities.

Another significant event in Dominica's calendar is Creole Day, celebrated on the last Friday in October. Creole Day is a day to celebrate the island's Creole culture and heritage, with people dressing in traditional Creole attire, speaking Creole language, and enjoying Creole cuisine and music. The streets come alive with vibrant colors, music, and dance, as communities across the island come together to honor their shared heritage.

Harvest festivals are also an important part of Dominican culture, with communities gathering to give thanks for the bounty of the land and sea. The Feast of Our Lady of Fatima, celebrated in the village of La Plaine in October, is one such festival, featuring religious processions, cultural performances, and a traditional boat race known as the Yole. The festival highlights the importance of agriculture and fishing in Dominican life and pays homage to the island's natural abundance.

Throughout the year, Dominica also celebrates various cultural events and holidays, including Emancipation Day, Independence Day, and the World Creole Music Festival. These events showcase the diversity of Dominican culture and provide opportunities for people to come together, celebrate, and honor their shared heritage.

In addition to religious and cultural festivals, Dominica is known for its traditional music and dance events, such as Quadrille and Lapo Kabwit. Quadrille is a lively dance performed to the accompaniment of accordion and drum music, while Lapo Kabwit is a traditional goatskin drumming ceremony performed during Easter celebrations and other special occasions.

Overall, traditional festivals and celebrations play a vital role in Dominican life, providing opportunities for people to come together, celebrate their cultural heritage, and strengthen community bonds. From religious observances to harvest festivals to music and dance events, these festivals showcase the unique identity and spirit of the Dominican people.

Dominica's Literary Heritage: Writers and Poets from the Nature Isle

Dominica's literary heritage is as rich and diverse as the island's natural beauty. From the lush rainforests to the rugged coastlines, Dominica has inspired generations of writers and poets to capture its essence in words. The island's literary tradition is a testament to its cultural richness and the creativity of its people.

One of Dominica's most celebrated literary figures is Jean Rhys, whose novel "Wide Sargasso Sea" is considered a classic of Caribbean literature. Born in Dominica in 1890, Rhys spent much of her life in England, but her experiences growing up on the island greatly influenced her writing. "Wide Sargasso Sea" is a prequel to Charlotte Brontë's "Jane Eyre" and explores themes of colonialism, identity, and racial inequality through the eyes of the character Bertha Mason, the "madwoman in the attic."

Another prominent Dominican writer is Phyllis Shand Allfrey, whose novel "The Orchid House" is set in Dominica during the period of colonial rule. Published in 1953, "The Orchid House" is a sweeping family saga that explores themes of race, class, and social change against the backdrop of the island's lush landscape. Allfrey was also a journalist and political activist, advocating for social justice and equality in the Caribbean.

Poetry has also flourished in Dominica, with poets such as Derek Walcott and Edward "Kamau" Brathwaite making significant contributions to Caribbean literature. Walcott, who was born in Saint Lucia but spent time in Dominica, won the Nobel Prize in Literature in 1992 for his epic poem "Omeros," which draws inspiration from Homer's "The Iliad" and "The Odyssey" to explore the complexities of Caribbean identity and history.

Kamau Brathwaite, born in Barbados but deeply connected to Dominica through his family roots, is known for his experimental poetry and his exploration of Caribbean folklore and mythology. His collection "The Arrivants: A New World Trilogy" is considered a landmark work in Caribbean literature, blending elements of African, Indian, and indigenous cultures to create a uniquely Caribbean poetic voice.

In addition to these well-known writers, Dominica has also produced a wealth of emerging talent in literature and poetry. Organizations such as the Nature Island Literary

Festival and Book Fair provide opportunities for writers and poets to showcase their work and connect with audiences both locally and internationally.

Overall, Dominica's literary heritage is a testament to the power of storytelling and the enduring influence of the island's natural beauty and cultural richness. From Jean Rhys to Phyllis Shand Allfrey to Derek Walcott and beyond, the writers and poets of Dominica continue to inspire and captivate readers with their words, offering a glimpse into the soul of the Nature Isle.

Visual Arts in Dominica: From Carib Petroglyphs to Contemporary Creations

Dominica's visual arts scene is as diverse and vibrant as the island's natural landscapes. From ancient Carib petroglyphs to contemporary creations, the art of Dominica reflects the island's rich cultural heritage and the creativity of its people.

One of the earliest forms of visual art in Dominica is found in the ancient petroglyphs carved by the island's indigenous Carib people. These intricate rock carvings depict scenes of everyday life, religious rituals, and symbols of spiritual significance, providing a window into the world of the island's earliest inhabitants.

European colonization brought new influences to Dominica's visual arts, with colonial-era paintings and sculptures reflecting the tastes and styles of the European elite. Many of these artworks can be found in churches, government buildings, and private collections throughout the island, offering insights into the colonial history and cultural exchange that shaped Dominica.

In the 20th century, Dominican artists began to explore new forms of expression, drawing inspiration from the island's natural beauty, cultural traditions, and social issues. One of the most notable figures in Dominica's modern art scene is Earl Etienne, whose vibrant paintings capture the colors and rhythms of Caribbean life. Etienne's work often features bold brushstrokes, vivid colors, and scenes of everyday life in Dominica, from bustling marketplaces to tranquil seaside vistas.

Another prominent Dominican artist is Patricia Pinard, whose sculptures and installations explore themes of identity, memory, and the environment. Pinard's work often incorporates found objects, natural materials, and traditional craft techniques, reflecting her commitment to sustainability and cultural preservation.

In addition to individual artists, Dominica is also home to a thriving community of artisans and craftspeople who create a wide range of handmade goods, from pottery and ceramics to jewelry and textiles. Many of these artisans draw inspiration from traditional Dominican crafts such as basket weaving, woodcarving, and pottery, infusing their work with a contemporary flair.

In recent years, Dominica's visual arts scene has continued to evolve and expand, with new galleries, studios, and art spaces opening across the island. Organizations such as the Dominica Arts and Crafts Association (DACA) and the Dominica Institute of the Arts (DIA) support local artists and promote cultural exchange through exhibitions, workshops, and community events.

Whether exploring ancient petroglyphs, admiring colonial-era paintings, or discovering contemporary creations, the visual arts of Dominica offer a glimpse into the island's past, present, and future. From Carib traditions to modern masterpieces, the art of Dominica celebrates the beauty, diversity, and creativity of the Nature Isle.

The Language of Dominica: Creole, English, and Multilingualism

The language landscape of Dominica is as diverse as its cultural heritage, reflecting a blend of influences from Africa, Europe, and the Caribbean. While English is the official language of Dominica, the island is also home to a vibrant Creole language known as Dominican Creole or Kweyol.

Dominican Creole is a creole language that emerged during the colonial era as a means of communication among enslaved Africans, indigenous Caribs, and European settlers. It is characterized by its unique vocabulary, grammar, and pronunciation, drawing heavily from West African languages such as Igbo, Yoruba, and Twi, as well as French, Spanish, and English.

Despite the dominance of English in government, education, and media, Dominican Creole remains widely spoken and is an important marker of cultural identity for many Dominicans. It is used in everyday communication, informal settings, and cultural expressions such as music, dance, and storytelling.

In addition to English and Dominican Creole, Dominica is also home to a diverse range of languages spoken by immigrant communities and descendants of indentured laborers from other

Caribbean islands and beyond. These include French, Spanish, Hindi, and various African languages, reflecting the island's history of migration and cultural exchange.

Multilingualism is common in Dominica, with many people growing up speaking two or more languages fluently. This linguistic diversity is celebrated and embraced as a reflection of the island's multicultural heritage and the spirit of unity in diversity that defines Dominican society.

In recent years, efforts have been made to promote and preserve Dominican Creole as a vital part of the island's cultural heritage. Organizations such as the Dominica Language Project and the Dominica Cultural Division support research, education, and advocacy initiatives aimed at raising awareness about the importance of Creole language and culture.

Overall, the language of Dominica reflects the island's complex history and cultural diversity, with English, Dominican Creole, and multilingualism serving as symbols of resilience, identity, and unity among the people of the Nature Isle.

Education in Dominica: Nurturing Minds, Shaping Futures

Education in Dominica is a cornerstone of the nation's development, providing opportunities for individuals to develop their skills, knowledge, and talents to contribute to society. The education system in Dominica is based on the British model, with primary, secondary, and tertiary levels of education.

At the primary level, education is compulsory for children between the ages of 5 and 16. Primary schools in Dominica are government-funded and provide education from kindergarten through to grade 6. The curriculum covers a range of subjects, including mathematics, science, language arts, social studies, and physical education.

Secondary education in Dominica begins at age 11 and continues until age 18. Secondary schools offer a comprehensive curriculum designed to prepare students for further education or employment. In addition to core academic subjects, students have the opportunity to study vocational subjects such as agriculture, home economics, and technical drawing.

The Caribbean Examinations Council (CXC) administers the Caribbean Secondary Education

Certificate (CSEC) examination, which is taken by students at the end of their secondary education. The CSEC is a nationally recognized qualification that opens doors to further education and employment opportunities.

For students who wish to pursue higher education, Dominica is home to the Dominica State College (DSC), which offers a range of associate and bachelor's degree programs in fields such as business, education, nursing, and environmental science. The DSC also offers technical and vocational training programs to prepare students for careers in areas such as hospitality, agriculture, and construction.

In addition to formal education, Dominica also places a strong emphasis on lifelong learning and adult education. The Adult Education Division of the Ministry of Education offers literacy and skills training programs for adults who wish to improve their education and employment prospects.

Despite its commitment to education, Dominica faces challenges in providing equal access to quality education for all its citizens. The island's rugged terrain and scattered population make it difficult to reach remote communities, while limited resources and infrastructure pose obstacles to educational development.

Nevertheless, the government of Dominica continues to invest in education and human capital development as a priority. Efforts are underway to improve school facilities, train and retain qualified teachers, and enhance the quality and relevance of the curriculum to meet the needs of a rapidly changing world.

Overall, education in Dominica plays a crucial role in shaping the future of the nation, empowering individuals to reach their full potential and contribute to the social, economic, and cultural development of the Nature Isle.

Religion in Dominica: A Tapestry of Faiths and Beliefs

Religion in Dominica is a vibrant and diverse tapestry, reflecting the island's multicultural heritage and the influence of various faiths and beliefs brought by settlers, missionaries, and immigrants over the centuries. The predominant religion in Dominica is Christianity, with the Roman Catholic Church being the largest denomination.

Catholicism was introduced to Dominica by European colonizers during the colonial period and remains a significant force in the island's religious landscape. The Catholic Church plays a central role in the lives of many Dominicans, with Catholicism deeply intertwined with cultural traditions and practices.

In addition to Catholicism, Protestantism is also widely practiced in Dominica, with various Protestant denominations such as Anglicanism, Methodism, and Pentecostalism having a significant presence on the island. These Protestant churches have their own distinct traditions, beliefs, and practices, but they all share a common commitment to spreading the Christian gospel and serving the community.

Alongside Christianity, other religions are also represented in Dominica, including Hinduism,

Islam, and Rastafarianism. Hinduism was brought to Dominica by indentured laborers from India in the 19th century and is practiced by a small but vibrant community on the island. Islam is practiced by a small number of Dominican Muslims, who trace their roots to immigrants from the Middle East and South Asia. Rastafarianism, which originated in Jamaica, has also found a following in Dominica, particularly among those who identify with its message of social justice, spirituality, and African heritage.

In addition to organized religion, Dominica is also home to various spiritual practices and belief systems rooted in indigenous and African traditions. These include spiritual healing, herbal medicine, and rituals honoring ancestors and nature spirits. While not officially recognized as religions, these practices play an important role in the lives of many Dominicans and contribute to the island's cultural diversity and spiritual richness.

Overall, religion in Dominica is characterized by its diversity, tolerance, and syncretism, with different faiths and beliefs coexisting and influencing one another in a dynamic and ever-evolving tapestry of faith. Whether through churches, temples, mosques, or sacred sites in nature, religion continues to be an integral part of Dominican life, providing comfort, community, and spiritual guidance to people of all backgrounds and walks of life.

Healthcare System in Dominica: Providing Care in Paradise

The healthcare system in Dominica is essential for providing medical care and services to the population of the island. While Dominica is known for its natural beauty and tranquil lifestyle, the healthcare infrastructure plays a crucial role in ensuring the well-being of residents and visitors alike.

The healthcare system in Dominica is primarily publicly funded and operated by the government through the Ministry of Health, Wellness, and New Health Investment. The Ministry oversees a network of healthcare facilities across the island, including hospitals, health centers, and clinics, which provide a range of medical services to the population.

Princess Margaret Hospital, located in the capital city of Roseau, is the main hospital in Dominica and serves as the primary referral center for medical emergencies and specialized care. The hospital offers a wide range of services, including emergency care, surgery, maternity services, and outpatient clinics, and is staffed by qualified medical professionals, including doctors, nurses, and specialists.

In addition to Princess Margaret Hospital, Dominica has several health centers and clinics located in rural and remote areas, providing primary healthcare services to communities outside of Roseau. These health centers offer general medical care, preventive services, maternal and child health services, and immunizations, among other services, and play a vital role in promoting health and wellness in underserved areas.

Despite its relatively small size and limited resources, the healthcare system in Dominica is committed to providing quality care to all residents, regardless of their ability to pay. The government of Dominica subsidizes healthcare services, making them affordable and accessible to the entire population.

In recent years, efforts have been made to improve and modernize the healthcare system in Dominica, including investments in infrastructure, equipment, and training programs for healthcare professionals. The government has also prioritized initiatives to promote preventive care, combat non-communicable diseases, and address the health needs of vulnerable populations, such as the elderly and those living in poverty.

In addition to public healthcare services, Dominica also has a growing private healthcare sector, with private hospitals, clinics, and medical practices offering a range of specialized services and treatments to those who can afford them. While the private sector plays a complementary role in the healthcare system, the government remains committed to ensuring that all residents have access to essential healthcare services, regardless of their socioeconomic status.

Overall, the healthcare system in Dominica is an essential component of the island's infrastructure, providing care and support to the population and contributing to the overall health and well-being of the Nature Isle. Despite challenges and limitations, the healthcare system continues to evolve and adapt to meet the needs of a changing society, ensuring that healthcare remains a priority in paradise.

Transportation in Dominica: Navigating the Island's Roads and Waters

Transportation in Dominica is a crucial aspect of everyday life, connecting communities, facilitating commerce, and enabling travel across the island's rugged terrain. Due to its mountainous landscape and winding roads, Dominica's transportation infrastructure presents unique challenges and opportunities for both locals and visitors alike.

One of the primary modes of transportation in Dominica is the road network, which consists of a network of paved and unpaved roads that crisscross the island. While the main roads are well-maintained and suitable for vehicular traffic, many secondary roads are narrow, steep, and prone to erosion, requiring careful navigation, particularly in rural areas.

Cars, vans, and buses are the most common forms of transportation on the island, providing essential services for commuting, shopping, and accessing healthcare and education facilities. Public transportation, operated by privately owned minibusses, known locally as "buses," serves as a lifeline for many Dominicans, offering affordable and accessible transportation services throughout the island.

In addition to road transportation, water transportation also plays a significant role in Dominica's transportation system, particularly for inter-island travel and tourism. The island's ports and harbors serve as gateways for cargo ships, ferries, and cruise ships, connecting Dominica to neighboring islands and international markets.

The main port of entry for sea transportation in Dominica is the Roseau Cruise Ship Berth, located in the capital city of Roseau. This modern facility accommodates cruise ships of all sizes and serves as a hub for tourism and economic activity on the island.

In recent years, efforts have been made to improve and expand Dominica's transportation infrastructure to meet the growing demands of a developing economy and tourism industry. Projects such as the rehabilitation of roads, construction of new bridges, and expansion of airport facilities have helped to enhance connectivity and accessibility across the island.

Air transportation in Dominica is facilitated by the Douglas-Charles Airport, located on the northeast coast of the island. Formerly known as

Melville Hall Airport, this airport serves as the main gateway for domestic and international flights, connecting Dominica to destinations throughout the Caribbean and beyond.

While Dominica's transportation system faces challenges such as limited resources, rugged terrain, and vulnerability to natural disasters, it also presents opportunities for innovation and sustainable development. Initiatives such as eco-friendly transportation options, community-based tourism projects, and investments in renewable energy infrastructure are helping to shape the future of transportation in Dominica, ensuring that it remains an integral part of life on the Nature Isle.

Sustainable Tourism in Dominica: Balancing Preservation and Progress

Sustainable tourism in Dominica is not just a buzzword; it's a guiding principle that shapes the island's approach to travel and hospitality. Known as the "Nature Isle of the Caribbean," Dominica is renowned for its pristine landscapes, diverse ecosystems, and rich cultural heritage, making it a magnet for eco-conscious travelers seeking authentic experiences in harmony with nature.

At the heart of sustainable tourism in Dominica is the concept of responsible travel, which emphasizes minimizing negative impacts on the environment, supporting local communities, and preserving cultural heritage. The government of Dominica, in collaboration with local stakeholders and international partners, has implemented various initiatives to promote sustainable tourism practices and ensure the long-term viability of the industry.

One of the pillars of sustainable tourism in Dominica is eco-friendly accommodations, including eco-lodges, guesthouses, and eco-resorts that are designed and operated with a focus on environmental conservation and community engagement. These properties often use renewable energy sources, practice water conservation and waste management, and offer educational programs to guests about local culture and environmental conservation.

In addition to eco-friendly accommodations, sustainable tourism in Dominica also encompasses a range of nature-based activities and experiences that allow visitors to explore the island's natural beauty while minimizing their ecological footprint. From hiking through lush rainforests and snorkeling in pristine coral reefs to birdwatching, whale watching, and visiting protected areas such as Morne Trois Pitons National Park, Dominica offers a wealth of opportunities for eco-conscious travelers to connect with nature in a responsible and respectful manner.

Community-based tourism initiatives are also a key component of sustainable tourism in Dominica, providing opportunities for local communities to participate in and benefit from the tourism industry. Homestays, guided tours led by local guides, and cultural experiences such as cooking classes and artisan workshops allow visitors to engage directly with Dominican culture and support local livelihoods.

Education and awareness are essential aspects of sustainable tourism in Dominica, with efforts underway to educate both visitors and locals about the importance of environmental conservation, cultural preservation, and responsible travel practices. Sustainable tourism certification programs, environmental education initiatives, and community outreach programs help to raise awareness and foster a culture of sustainability among all stakeholders.

Despite its commitment to sustainable tourism, Dominica faces challenges such as limited infrastructure, vulnerability to natural disasters, and competition from larger, more developed destinations in the Caribbean. However, through strategic planning, collaboration, and innovation, Dominica continues to pave the way forward as a leader in sustainable tourism, demonstrating that it is possible to balance preservation and progress for the benefit of both people and the planet.

Eco-Tourism Adventures: Hiking, Canyoning, and Nature Trails

Embarking on eco-tourism adventures in Dominica is like stepping into a natural playground where every trail, waterfall, and canyon beckons with the promise of adventure and discovery. Hiking is one of the most popular activities for nature enthusiasts, with a network of trails crisscrossing the island's diverse landscapes. From the challenging ascent of Morne Diablotin, the highest peak in Dominica, to leisurely strolls through the lush rainforests of the Syndicate Nature Trail, there are hiking options for every skill level and interest.

For those seeking an adrenaline rush, canyoning offers a thrilling way to explore Dominica's rugged terrain. Guided canyoning tours take adventurers through narrow gorges, cascading waterfalls, and natural rock formations, offering opportunities for rappelling, swimming, and scrambling over boulders. The Titou Gorge and the Emerald Pool are popular canyoning destinations, where visitors can plunge into crystal-clear pools and swim through narrow passages carved by ancient rivers.

Nature trails are another eco-friendly way to experience Dominica's natural wonders. Whether wandering through the Botanical Gardens in

Roseau, exploring the Kalinago Barana Aute Cultural Village, or birdwatching along the Syndicate Nature Trail, nature trails provide opportunities for visitors to immerse themselves in the island's biodiversity while learning about its cultural heritage.

One of the highlights of eco-tourism adventures in Dominica is the Waitukubuli National Trail, a 115-mile hiking trail that traverses the length of the island from Scotts Head in the south to Cabrits National Park in the north. Divided into 14 segments, the Waitukubuli National Trail showcases the diversity of Dominica's landscapes, from coastal cliffs and volcanic peaks to lush valleys and pristine rivers.

In addition to hiking, canyoning, and nature trails, eco-tourism adventures in Dominica also include activities such as birdwatching, whale watching, snorkeling, and diving. Dominica is home to over 170 species of birds, including the rare and endemic Sisserou parrot, making it a paradise for birdwatchers. Whale watching tours offer the chance to see sperm whales, pilot whales, and dolphins in their natural habitat, while snorkeling and diving enthusiasts can explore vibrant coral reefs, underwater caves, and marine life in marine reserves such as the Soufriere Scotts Head Marine Reserve.

Overall, eco-tourism adventures in Dominica offer a unique blend of outdoor recreation, cultural immersion, and environmental education, providing visitors with unforgettable experiences while contributing to the conservation and sustainable development of the Nature Isle. Whether hiking through the rainforest, rappelling down waterfalls, or snorkeling in crystal-clear waters, eco-tourism adventures in Dominica are sure to leave a lasting impression on adventurers of all ages and backgrounds.

Hot Springs and Wellness Tourism: Relaxation and Rejuvenation in Dominica

Hot springs and wellness tourism in Dominica offer visitors a serene escape into the island's natural healing wonders. Nestled amidst the lush rainforests and volcanic landscapes, Dominica's hot springs are revered for their therapeutic properties and tranquil surroundings. Boiling Lake, one of the world's largest hot springs and a UNESCO World Heritage Site, draws adventurers to its mist-shrouded crater, where the steam rises from the bubbling waters below, creating an otherworldly ambiance.

The island boasts numerous hot springs, each with its own unique charm and healing benefits. Tucked away in the heart of the Morne Trois Pitons National Park, the Wotten Waven hot springs offer a secluded oasis for relaxation and rejuvenation. Visitors can soak in natural pools fed by warm mineral-rich waters, surrounded by verdant foliage and the soothing sounds of nature.

Another popular hot spring destination in Dominica is the Screw's Sulphur Spa, located near the village of Trafalgar. This historic spa has been welcoming visitors for centuries, offering therapeutic mud baths, mineral baths, and steam rooms infused with the natural healing properties of sulfur and other minerals. The warm waters of the spa are said to soothe sore muscles, relieve joint pain, and promote overall wellness.

In addition to hot springs, wellness tourism in Dominica encompasses a range of holistic health and wellness practices aimed at nurturing the mind, body, and spirit. Yoga retreats, meditation workshops, and spa treatments are popular offerings for visitors seeking relaxation and self-care. The island's serene natural surroundings provide the perfect backdrop for mindfulness practices and holistic healing therapies.

Dominica's wellness tourism industry also includes eco-friendly resorts, wellness retreats, and eco-lodges that cater to health-conscious travelers seeking sustainable and environmentally friendly accommodations. These properties often offer organic farm-to-table dining, yoga and wellness classes, and eco-friendly amenities designed to promote well-being and mindfulness.

Beyond hot springs and wellness retreats, Dominica's natural beauty and biodiversity provide countless opportunities for outdoor recreation and adventure. From hiking through rainforests and waterfalls to snorkeling in pristine coral reefs and kayaking down winding rivers, visitors to Dominica can immerse themselves in nature while nourishing their body and soul.

Overall, hot springs and wellness tourism in Dominica offer a holistic approach to health and relaxation, inviting visitors to unwind, recharge, and connect with the healing power of nature. Whether soaking in a natural hot spring, practicing yoga in the rainforest, or indulging in a spa treatment, wellness seekers will find a sanctuary of serenity and rejuvenation on the Nature Isle.

Dominica's Unique Accommodation: Eco-Lodges, Guesthouses, and Villas

Dominica's accommodation options offer travelers a unique opportunity to immerse themselves in the island's natural beauty and rich culture. From eco-lodges nestled in the rainforest to charming guesthouses overlooking the Caribbean Sea, there's a lodging option to suit every taste and budget.

Eco-lodges are a popular choice for travelers seeking sustainable and environmentally friendly accommodations. These lodges are often built using locally sourced materials and designed to blend harmoniously with the surrounding environment. Many eco-lodges in Dominica are powered by renewable energy sources such as solar panels and hydroelectric generators, minimizing their carbon footprint and impact on the environment.

Guesthouses are another popular accommodation option in Dominica, offering travelers a more intimate and authentic experience. Run by local families, guesthouses provide a glimpse into Dominican life and culture, with personalized service and insider knowledge of the island's hidden gems. Guests can expect warm hospitality, home-cooked meals, and a chance to connect with the local community. For travelers seeking luxury and privacy, villas and vacation rentals offer an exclusive retreat amidst Dominica's natural splendor. From cliff-top villas with panoramic ocean views to secluded cottages tucked away in the rainforest, these accommodations provide a tranquil oasis for relaxation and rejuvenation. Many villas come equipped with private pools, outdoor living spaces, and modern amenities, ensuring a comfortable and memorable stay.

One of the advantages of staying in eco-lodges, guesthouses, and villas in Dominica is the opportunity to experience the island's natural wonders up close. Many accommodations are located near hiking trails, waterfalls, and beaches, allowing guests to explore the island's diverse landscapes at their own pace. Some eco-lodges even offer guided tours and eco-friendly activities such as birdwatching, snorkeling, and sustainable farming experiences.

In recent years, the trend towards eco-friendly and sustainable tourism has led to an increase in the number of eco-lodges, guesthouses, and villas in Dominica. These accommodations cater to travelers who prioritize environmental conservation, cultural authenticity, and responsible travel practices. By choosing to stay in eco-friendly accommodations, visitors can support local communities, preserve natural resources, and minimize their impact on the environment while enjoying a truly unforgettable experience on the Nature Isle.

Shopping and Souvenirs: Authentic Crafts and Local Products

Shopping for authentic crafts and local products in Dominica is a delightful experience that allows visitors to bring a piece of the island's rich culture and heritage home with them. From vibrant markets bustling with activity to quaint boutiques tucked away in colonial buildings, there are plenty of opportunities to discover unique souvenirs and treasures while exploring the island.

One of the best places to start your shopping adventure in Dominica is the Roseau Market, located in the heart of the capital city. Here, you'll find a vibrant array of stalls selling everything from fresh produce and spices to handmade crafts and souvenirs. Be sure to explore the craft market section, where local artisans showcase their talents with intricately woven baskets, colorful batik fabrics, and hand-carved wooden sculptures.

For those interested in traditional Dominican crafts, a visit to the Kalinago Barana Aute Cultural Village is a must. This indigenous community offers a glimpse into the island's pre-Columbian heritage, with demonstrations of traditional craft techniques such as pottery making, basket weaving, and canoe carving. Visitors can purchase authentic handmade crafts directly from the artisans, supporting the local economy and preserving indigenous traditions.

Dominica is also known for its vibrant arts scene, with many local artists showcasing their work in galleries and studios throughout the island. From paintings and sculptures to ceramics and jewelry, there's something for every art lover to admire and collect. Look for pieces that capture the essence of Dominica's natural beauty, from scenes of lush rainforests and cascading waterfalls to vibrant tropical flora and fauna.

When it comes to local products, Dominica is renowned for its natural beauty and wellness offerings. Look for skincare products made with indigenous ingredients such as coconut oil, cocoa butter, and volcanic clay, which are known for their nourishing and healing properties. You'll also find a variety of herbal teas, spices, and condiments made from locally grown herbs and spices, perfect for adding a taste of Dominica to your culinary creations back home.

For a truly unique souvenir, consider purchasing a piece of Dominican art or craft that reflects the island's rich cultural heritage and natural beauty. Whether it's a handcrafted pottery piece, a woven basket, or a painting by a local artist, you'll be sure to treasure your Dominican souvenir for years to come, as a reminder of your unforgettable experience on the Nature Isle.

Environmental Conservation in Dominica: Protecting the Nature Island

Environmental conservation in Dominica is a top priority for both the government and local communities, as the island's pristine ecosystems are central to its identity as the "Nature Island of the Caribbean." With its lush rainforests, crystal-clear rivers, and vibrant coral reefs, Dominica boasts some of the most biodiverse landscapes in the region, teeming with rare and endemic species of flora and fauna.

One of the key initiatives for environmental conservation in Dominica is the establishment and management of protected areas. The island is home to several national parks, marine reserves, and forest reserves that safeguard critical habitats and wildlife populations. Morne Trois Pitons National Park, a UNESCO World Heritage Site, protects over 17,000 acres of pristine rainforest, volcanic peaks, and natural wonders such as the Boiling Lake and Trafalgar Falls.

In addition to protected areas, Dominica has implemented policies and regulations to promote sustainable land use and natural resource management. The Forestry, Wildlife, and

National Parks Act regulates logging, hunting, and other activities within forested areas, while the Fisheries Act governs fishing practices and marine conservation efforts. These laws are designed to balance the needs of local communities with the imperative to protect biodiversity and ecosystem health.

Community-based conservation initiatives play a crucial role in environmental stewardship in Dominica. Local organizations, such as the Waitukubuli Ecological Foundation and the Dominica Sustainable Tourism Association, work closely with communities to promote sustainable agriculture, reforestation, and eco-friendly practices. These initiatives empower communities to take ownership of their natural resources and contribute to conservation efforts on the ground.

Climate change poses a significant threat to Dominica's fragile ecosystems, exacerbating challenges such as sea-level rise, extreme weather events, and coral bleaching. In response, the government of Dominica has prioritized climate resilience and adaptation measures, including the development of climate-smart agriculture, renewable energy projects, and coastal protection strategies. International partnerships, such as the Global Climate Fund and the Caribbean Biodiversity Fund, provide financial and technical support for these initiatives.

Education and awareness are essential components of environmental conservation in Dominica, with efforts underway to engage youth, schools, and communities in environmental stewardship and sustainability practices. Environmental education programs, nature-based tourism experiences, and eco-tours offer opportunities for visitors and locals alike to learn about the importance of protecting the island's natural heritage.

Overall, environmental conservation in Dominica is a multifaceted endeavor that requires collaboration, innovation, and long-term commitment from all stakeholders. By safeguarding its natural resources and embracing sustainable development practices, Dominica is not only preserving its unique biodiversity but also ensuring a vibrant and resilient future for generations to come.

Community Development Initiatives in Dominica: Empowering Local Voices

Community development initiatives in Dominica are essential for fostering sustainable growth and empowering local voices in shaping the future of the island. With its diverse communities and rich cultural heritage, Dominica has a wealth of resources and potential that can be harnessed through community-driven projects and programs.

One of the key areas of focus for community development in Dominica is sustainable agriculture. Many rural communities rely on agriculture as a primary source of income, and initiatives such as organic farming, agroforestry, and community gardens are helping to improve food security, livelihoods, and environmental sustainability. Organizations like the Dominica Association of Rural Women (DARW) provide training and support to women farmers, empowering them to play a leading role in agricultural development and economic empowerment.

Education is another critical component of community development in Dominica. Access to quality education is essential for empowering individuals and communities to reach their full potential. The government of Dominica has made significant investments in education, including the construction of new schools, expansion of educational programs, and provision of scholarships and bursaries to students. Community-based organizations and non-profit groups also play a vital role in supporting educational initiatives, such as after-school programs, literacy campaigns, and vocational training opportunities.

Entrepreneurship and small business development are key drivers of economic growth and community empowerment in Dominica. Initiatives such as microfinance programs, business incubators, and skills training workshops help aspiring entrepreneurs and small business owners to start and grow their ventures. The Dominica Youth Business Trust (DYBT) provides mentorship, funding, and resources to young entrepreneurs, enabling them to turn their business ideas into reality and contribute to economic development in their communities.

Cultural preservation and heritage conservation are also important aspects of community development in Dominica. The island's rich cultural traditions, including music, dance, and art, are central to its identity and sense of belonging. Community-based cultural initiatives, such as heritage festivals, craft markets, and cultural heritage tours, celebrate and preserve Dominica's cultural heritage while providing economic opportunities for local artisans and performers.

Community resilience and disaster preparedness are critical considerations for community development in Dominica, given the island's vulnerability to natural hazards such as hurricanes, floods, and landslides. Community-based disaster risk reduction initiatives, such as early warning systems, emergency shelters, and disaster response training, help communities to prepare for and respond to emergencies, reducing the impact of disasters on lives and livelihoods.

Overall, community development initiatives in Dominica are driven by a commitment to empowering local communities, promoting social inclusion, and fostering sustainable development. By harnessing the creativity, resilience, and collective action of its people, Dominica is building a brighter future for all its citizens, one community at a time.

Disaster Preparedness and Resilience in Dominica: Facing Nature's Fury

Disaster preparedness and resilience are critical aspects of life in Dominica, a Caribbean island that faces the constant threat of natural disasters such as hurricanes, floods, and landslides. Situated in the hurricane belt, Dominica is particularly vulnerable to the devastating impact of tropical storms and hurricanes during the Atlantic hurricane season, which runs from June to November each year.

In recent decades, Dominica has experienced several major natural disasters that have tested the resilience of its people and infrastructure. Hurricane Maria, which struck the island in September 2017 as a Category 5 storm, caused widespread destruction, with winds exceeding 160 miles per hour and torrential rainfall triggering flash floods and mudslides. The hurricane caused extensive damage to homes, infrastructure, agriculture, and the environment, resulting in loss of life and livelihoods.

In the aftermath of Hurricane Maria, Dominica embarked on a comprehensive recovery and rebuilding effort aimed at enhancing disaster preparedness and resilience across the island.

The government, in partnership with international agencies and donors, implemented measures to strengthen infrastructure, improve early warning systems, and build community resilience to future disasters.

One of the key initiatives undertaken by the government of Dominica is the construction of resilient infrastructure, including reinforced buildings, storm-resistant shelters, and flood mitigation measures. The goal is to reduce the vulnerability of communities to the impact of hurricanes and other natural hazards, ensuring that critical infrastructure remains functional during and after disasters.

Early warning systems are essential for disaster preparedness in Dominica, providing timely alerts and information to residents about impending hazards such as hurricanes, floods, and landslides. The Dominica Meteorological Service, in collaboration with regional and international partners, monitors weather patterns and issues advisories and warnings to the public via radio, television, and social media platforms.

Community-based disaster preparedness initiatives play a vital role in building resilience at the grassroots level. Neighborhood watch groups, disaster response teams, and community emergency plans help communities to organize and coordinate their response to disasters, minimizing loss of life and property damage. Training programs in first aid, search and rescue, and disaster risk reduction equip residents with the skills and knowledge they need to protect themselves and others during emergencies.

In addition to physical infrastructure and early warning systems, disaster preparedness in Dominica also encompasses measures to safeguard the environment and natural resources. Reforestation efforts, watershed management programs, and sustainable land use practices help to reduce the risk of flooding, erosion, and landslides, while protecting biodiversity and ecosystem services.

Overall, disaster preparedness and resilience are ongoing priorities for Dominica, as the island continues to confront the challenges posed by climate change and natural hazards. By investing in resilient infrastructure, early warning systems, and community-based initiatives, Dominica is working to ensure the safety, security, and well-being of its citizens in the face of nature's fury.

Future Prospects for Dominica: Challenges and Opportunities Ahead

Looking ahead to the future, Dominica faces a mix of challenges and opportunities that will shape the trajectory of the island's development in the years to come. As a small island nation in the Caribbean, Dominica grapples with various socio-economic, environmental, and geopolitical factors that influence its prospects for growth and resilience.

One of the key challenges facing Dominica is its vulnerability to natural disasters and the impacts of climate change. The island's susceptibility to hurricanes, floods, and landslides poses significant risks to lives, livelihoods, and infrastructure. In recent years, Dominica has experienced several devastating hurricanes, including Hurricane Maria in 2017, highlighting the urgent need for enhanced disaster preparedness, resilience, and adaptation measures.

Economic diversification is another pressing issue for Dominica, as the island's economy remains heavily reliant on agriculture, tourism, and remittances. While these sectors contribute to the island's economy, they are vulnerable to external shocks and market fluctuations. The government of Dominica has identified sectors such as renewable energy, information technology, and ecotourism as potential areas for growth and investment, aiming to reduce dependency on traditional industries and create new opportunities for sustainable development.

Investment in infrastructure is essential for unlocking Dominica's economic potential and improving the quality of life for its citizens. The government has prioritized infrastructure projects such as road upgrades, port expansions, and renewable energy initiatives to enhance connectivity, promote trade and investment, and provide essential services to remote communities. International partnerships and financing mechanisms, such as grants, loans, and public-private partnerships, play a crucial role in funding these projects and supporting long-term development goals.

Education and human capital development are fundamental to Dominica's future prosperity, as they empower individuals and communities to thrive in a rapidly changing world. The government has invested in initiatives to improve access to quality education, training, and skills development opportunities, with a focus on promoting lifelong learning, innovation, and entrepreneurship. By equipping its citizens with the knowledge, skills, and capabilities needed to succeed in the global economy, Dominica aims to build a resilient and inclusive society that can adapt to emerging challenges and seize new opportunities.

Environmental conservation and sustainability are integral to Dominica's future prosperity and well-being. The island's rich biodiversity, pristine landscapes, and cultural heritage are valuable assets that must be protected and preserved for future generations. Dominica has committed to ambitious targets for environmental protection, climate action, and sustainable development, including the establishment of marine protected areas, reforestation efforts, and renewable energy initiatives. By embracing a holistic approach to sustainability, Dominica can safeguard its natural resources, mitigate the impacts of climate change, and promote resilience and prosperity for all.

In conclusion, the future of Dominica hinges on its ability to address challenges, harness opportunities, and chart a course toward sustainable development and resilience. By investing in infrastructure, education, environmental conservation, and economic diversification, Dominica can build a brighter and more prosperous future for its citizens and contribute to a more resilient and sustainable Caribbean region.

Cultural Exchange and Volunteerism: Connecting with Dominica's Communities

Cultural exchange and volunteerism play pivotal roles in fostering connections and understanding between visitors and the communities of Dominica. The island's rich cultural heritage, diverse traditions, and warm hospitality offer visitors unique opportunities to engage with local communities, learn about their way of life, and contribute positively to their development.

Volunteerism has long been a cornerstone of community engagement in Dominica, with local organizations and grassroots initiatives leading efforts to address social, environmental, and economic challenges. From community clean-up projects and youth mentorship programs to environmental conservation initiatives and disaster relief efforts, volunteers from around the world collaborate with local residents to make a difference in their communities. Organizations such as the Dominica Red Cross Society, the Nature Island Foundation, and the Waitukubuli Ecological Foundation provide platforms for volunteers to get involved in meaningful projects that benefit both local communities and the environment.

Cultural exchange programs offer visitors immersive experiences that allow them to connect with Dominica's vibrant culture and heritage. Homestays, cultural immersion tours, and community-based tourism initiatives provide opportunities for travelers to live and work alongside local residents, participate in traditional activities, and gain insights into the island's customs, beliefs, and way of life. Through hands-on experiences such as cooking classes, craft workshops, and music and dance performances, visitors can develop a deeper appreciation for Dominica's cultural diversity and strengthen bonds with the communities they visit.

One of the most impactful forms of cultural exchange and volunteerism in Dominica is through service-learning programs and international partnerships. Educational institutions, non-profit organizations, and governmental agencies collaborate on projects that address pressing social and environmental issues while providing valuable learning experiences for students and professionals. Whether conducting research on marine conservation, promoting health education in schools, or supporting community development initiatives, participants in these programs contribute their skills and expertise to meaningful projects that make a positive impact on the lives of Dominicans.

Volunteer tourism, also known as "voluntourism," is a growing trend in Dominica, with visitors combining leisure travel with volunteer work to make a difference in local communities. From teaching English in schools and assisting with sustainable agriculture projects to participating in eco-tourism activities and supporting small businesses, voluntourists engage in a wide range of activities that contribute to community development and cultural exchange. These experiences not only benefit local communities but also provide enriching and meaningful experiences for volunteers, fostering cross-cultural understanding and personal growth.

In conclusion, cultural exchange and volunteerism are powerful tools for connecting with Dominica's communities, fostering mutual understanding, and promoting sustainable development. By actively engaging with local residents, learning about their culture and way of life, and contributing to community-led initiatives, visitors can make a positive impact while creating memorable experiences that enrich their lives and the lives of others.

Tips for Traveling to Dominica: Practical Advice for a Memorable Trip

Traveling to Dominica offers a unique and unforgettable experience for adventurers seeking to explore the natural beauty, rich culture, and warm hospitality of the Nature Island. Whether you're planning a solo getaway, a romantic escape, or a family vacation, here are some practical tips to help you make the most of your trip:

1. **Travel Documents**: Ensure that you have a valid passport with at least six months of validity remaining before your planned departure date. Depending on your nationality, you may also need a visa to enter Dominica, so check the requirements well in advance.
2. **Health Precautions**: Visit your healthcare provider before traveling to Dominica to receive any necessary vaccinations or medications. Mosquito-borne illnesses such as dengue fever and Zika virus are present on the island, so be sure to pack insect repellent and take precautions to avoid mosquito bites.
3. **Packing Essentials**: Pack light, breathable clothing suitable for warm

tropical weather, as well as sturdy hiking shoes or sandals for exploring the island's rugged terrain. Don't forget to bring sunscreen, a hat, sunglasses, and a reusable water bottle to stay hydrated during your adventures.
4. **Currency and Banking**: The official currency of Dominica is the Eastern Caribbean dollar (XCD), although U.S. dollars are widely accepted. ATMs are available in major towns and tourist areas, but it's a good idea to carry some cash for smaller purchases and establishments that may not accept cards.
5. **Language**: English is the official language of Dominica, but you'll also hear locals speaking Dominican Creole, a unique blend of English, French, and African languages. Learning a few basic phrases in Creole, such as "Bonjou" (good morning) and "Tanpri" (please), can enhance your interactions with locals.
6. **Transportation**: Getting around Dominica is relatively easy, with taxis, buses, and rental cars available for transportation. Keep in mind that roads can be narrow and winding, so if you choose to drive, exercise caution and be prepared for adventurous journeys through the island's lush landscapes.

7. **Safety and Security**: Dominica is generally a safe destination for travelers, but it's always wise to take precautions to protect yourself and your belongings. Avoid walking alone at night, stay informed about local safety conditions, and heed any warnings or advisories issued by local authorities.
8. **Responsible Tourism**: Respect the environment and local culture during your visit to Dominica by practicing responsible tourism. Support eco-friendly accommodations, minimize your environmental impact by reducing waste and conserving water, and engage with local communities in a respectful and culturally sensitive manner.
9. **Exploring Nature**: Dominica is renowned for its stunning natural attractions, including waterfalls, hot springs, and pristine rainforests. Be sure to visit iconic sites such as Trafalgar Falls, Boiling Lake, and Emerald Pool, and consider hiring a local guide for immersive nature tours and hiking adventures.
10. **Embracing the Culture**: Immerse yourself in Dominica's vibrant culture by attending local festivals, sampling traditional cuisine, and learning about the island's history and heritage. Don't be afraid to try local delicacies such as

"callaloo" (a leafy green soup) and "roti" (a savory pastry filled with meat or vegetables) for an authentic taste of Dominican cuisine.

By following these practical tips and embracing the spirit of adventure, you're sure to have a memorable and rewarding journey to Dominica, where every corner of the island holds the promise of discovery and wonder.

Epilogue

In the closing pages of this book, it's time to reflect on the journey we've taken together through the vibrant landscapes, rich culture, and fascinating history of Dominica. From the towering peaks of Morne Trois Pitons to the bustling streets of Roseau, we've explored the wonders of the Nature Island and delved into the stories of its people.

As we bid farewell to Dominica, it's clear that this small Caribbean nation holds a special place in the hearts of all who visit. Its lush rainforests, crystal-clear rivers, and diverse wildlife captivate the senses and leave a lasting impression on those who are fortunate enough to experience its beauty firsthand.

But beyond its natural splendor, Dominica is a land of resilience, community, and hope. From the challenges of colonization and slavery to the triumphs of independence and self-determination, the people of Dominica have endured and persevered, forging a unique identity that is as vibrant as the colors of its carnival celebrations.

As we turn the final page of this book, let us carry with us the lessons learned from Dominica's past and the inspiration drawn from its present. Let us remember the importance of preserving our natural environment, celebrating our cultural heritage, and nurturing the bonds of community that unite us all.

And so, as we say goodbye to Dominica, let us not bid farewell, but rather, "au revoir" - until we meet again. For the memories we've made and the experiences we've shared will live on in our hearts, reminding us always of the beauty and resilience of the Nature Island and its people.

Printed in Great Britain
by Amazon